Take Three: 2

AGNI is known for its strong commitment to publishing both established and upcoming writing talents. Founded by Askold Melnyczuk in 1972, AGNI has published poems, essays, and short fiction by American and international writers including Seamus Heaney, Margaret Atwood, Noam Chomsky, Yusef Komunyakaa, Derek Walcott, Susanna Kaysen, Robert Pinsky, and Sharon Olds. AGNI is dedicated to bringing voices together in a magazine Joyce Carol Oates says is "known for commitment not only to work of consistently high quality but to thematic subjects of crucial and lasting significance." *Take Three: 2* is the second in an important annual series designed to launch the work of young poets chosen by AGNI's editorial board. *Take Three: 1* featured the poetry of Thomas Sayers Ellis, Larisa Szporluk, and Joe Osterhaus.

Take Three: 2

AGNI *New Poets Series*

GRAYWOLF PRESS

Publication of this volume is made possible in part by a grant
provided by the Minnesota State Arts Board through an
appropriation by the Minnesota State Legislature, and by
a grant from the National Endowment for the Arts. Significant
additional support has been provided by the Andrew W. Mellon
Foundation, the Lila Wallace-Reader's Digest Fund, the McKnight
Foundation, and other generous contributions from foundations,
corporations, and individuals. To these organizations and indi-
viduals who make our work possible, we offer heartfelt thanks.

Published by Graywolf Press
2402 University Avenue, Suite 203
Saint Paul, Minnesota 55114

Printed in the United States of America.

ISBN 1-55597-254-3

2   4   6   8   9   7   5   3   1
First Graywolf Printing, 1997

Library of Congress Catalog Card Number: 96-78739

Take Three: 2 was supported by a grant
from the Eric Mathieu King Fund of
The Academy of American Poets.

Susan Aizenberg

Peru

SUSAN AIZENBERG was born in Brooklyn, New York, and has lived also in Nevada, Connecticut, upstate New York, Texas, Florida, and for the past ten years, Nebraska. Her poems have appeared in many journals, including *AGNI, Prairie Schooner, The Journal,* and *Laurel Review*. Currently she is Poetry Editor of the *Nebraska Review* and teaches part-time in the Writer's Workshop at the University of Nebraska in Omaha.

for my family

Being arches itself   over the vast abyss.
Ah, the ball that we dared,   that we hurled into infinite space,
doesn't it fill our hands   differently with its return:
heavier by the weight   of where it has been.

RAINER MARIA RILKE

I

Cortland, 1970

Always Monday, light October drizzle
misting our hair, wet-
wool musk of our pea coats.
Remember your father's library?
Three-for-a-buck novels,

all the rosy *headlights*
he could dream, group-gropes he couldn't.
Breakfast was beer in a jelly
glass. Then the ten-block walk,
hardscrabble shacks

imploding, to swing shift
at Smith-Corona. I still have the scar
acid etched through my jeans
that first night. Peeling them down
in the Ladies Room, I found a black

circle the size of a quarter.
In May we married between small claims
and traffic courts, my mother
sweating in cheap mink, the best man
sniffling, aching to get straight.

Art

. . . ordinary isn't possible anymore
ADAM ZAGAJEWSKI

In the teachers' lounge, the tall, pretty
Irish woman tells me her anorexic
daughter's been hospitalized two years.
She's fifteen. Their debts are something she can
only laugh about. I sip tepid coffee,
tell her about the afternoon I watched
deputies cuff my son, pat him down
against a black and white while he invited
them to *suck his cock, fuck him in the ass,*
and cried. Today, I teach figurative
constructions to high school juniors signed up
for creative writing in hope of an easy grade.
I quote Wallace Stevens, wonder
what metaphor I can use to find the unities
in this: what was he *like* raging by that car?
Was the sun *fiery*? The police faces
stone? Soon, I'll speak to English teachers
from four schools about the value of "art
and imagination" to students whose twelve-step
stories of locked wards and halfway-house
failures I've listened to all week.
I don't know what to say about these stories,
how to explain that they come to me daily,
as if I wear some sign. And I don't know
what it means, as I watch them laughing
in school hallways, slamming their lockers,
tonguing each other in a sweet approximation
of love. When I call him at the hospital,
my son tells me a story: a friend
has died, the rumor is someone scotchgarded
his dope. Forgive me if this seems

extreme—I don't know how to make things
ordinary anymore, though I dress and go to work
each day as if the world were ordinary,
as if our lives might unfurl easily as some
well-mannered plot—carefully
rounded characters strolling bucolic paths,
safe beneath lucid trees, their steps
measured and graceful as the orderly
progression of their lives—a shapeliness
such as no one might imagine anymore.

The Women in Your Poems

Like inflatable lovers breasting
display windows in the shops on Times Square,

the women in your poems can't forgive
you for making them so beautiful.

You're growing tired of the way they leave you,
rising from your desk on clear syllable

balloons, floating through a window
in your mind to blossom, evening lychnis,

on your imaginary front lawn.
Pockets filled with scrap paper,

you cruise the gunmetal streets of a New York
winter, listening at alleyways

for the echo of their voices,
whispering *angel*, calling you *friend*.

The Life You Really Have

. . . the trees are trying to tell me things
I don't want to hear.
RICHARD JACKSON

These days each thing speaks
to you, but their languages, thank God,
are untranslatable.
Its voice vaguely sinister,
as if it were about to laugh,
your house murmurs
something about quiet and safety.
Even carpeting, thick as the despair

of the middle class,
can't muffle its whisper.
It's not like those voices K
heard, fabulous shapes in the air
calling her toward a rope,
the kitchen chair turned over. She heard
the dial tone hiss like a rattler,
woke to Thorazine, restraint. No,

it's more the hum of traffic
and conversation you hear on certain
afternoons, standing on some corner,
maybe in front of the library,
the post office, how each sound
swells into a moment when you don't know
who you are. You're just a woman
standing on the street,

listening to the trees, the day
sunny, or not. You're wearing what
you're wearing, your hair is how it is,

and when you look down
to see the shape of your body,
the particular angle of your shadow or
its absence, everything adds up
to someone familiar who

could be anyone, have any
of those lives you didn't choose —
another man, or no man.
And possibly it's the sound
of laughter, after all, the audience
a little drunk and sorrowful,
the ancient joke
you finally understand.

Luminous Child

The patient will not speak
except to say *tomato, broom, fire.*
Anger appears to be a major issue in this case.
Mother's history reveals
a fascination with certain wrong-way
streets, the rumpled sheets
of backroom cots, an edgy desire
for loss common to compulsive
gamblers. Patient manifests an obsessive
fantasy concerning *the dark lakes*
of Peru where in dreams
he's a white light, a bullet
plunging deep through water the red sheen
of Beaujolais. He's an infant,
pearly and round, tracing the rapid
downshift of a free fall no mother
can catch. Patient denies
any memory of riding through November
yellows, Dallas, the back
of his mother's bike, sipping air
sweet with lilac, speed
carrying them both through streets
blurred with color, her hair windy
and soft in his face, the familiar arc
of her neck and back between him
and whatever came on. He would like
to confess the theft of his
mother's pearl ring, gift for a girl
whose hair kinked and roiled
like Janis Joplin's in the photograph
on his mother's album, Big Brother
and the Holding Company, like bikers,

his gone father, he thinks. He can no more
explain his need than that luminous child
spiraling through Peruvian dream
waters can explain his, or you, yours.
Me, mine.

Grace

From the next-door court, the echoing
      sounds of a game, pickup basketball,
men shouting and the sweet, rocking
      harmonies of "I Second That Emotion,"

amped up loud and slightly tinny
      on a cheap cassette, joyous all the same.
Someone, mercifully, has killed
      the fluorescent overheads and lifted

the shades, and now this small gym
      floats in a dazzle of sunlight,
our repeating images, sweat-suited women
      and men, my own glistening skin,

lost in the brilliant glare
      reflecting off the mirrored wall.
There is no other world than this one,
      I believe it. Simple enough

to conjure metaphor—stasis,
      entrapment—from this rote walk
to nowhere, this treadmill with its queer,
      spongy belt endlessly cycling,

pale numbers for time passed,
      for distance traveled only
in the digital imagination of its computer,
      pulsing calmly through the black sheen

of its blind face—me,
      panting to slim my forty-year-old body,
toughen my aging heart. But this morning,
      I can almost believe anything

is possible, this world,
    with its intricate and mutable
geographies, so many restless
    players weaving the extraordinary

stories of their lives,
    is enough. I'm not saying it's more
than this luminous September sky,
    a feeling transitory as the good

chill through our window,
    where hours ago, I woke to solace,
the small heat of your breath
    against my arm. Or that night's

relentless ghosts won't return
    to lead me, a dim and anxious student
of the cold, planetary dark,
    to that same window, unable to sleep.

Still, how lavish, even this
    momentary knowing, the past dissolving
to muscle and pulse, the autumn
    morning, this music filtering through.

for Jeffrey

II

Debut: Late Lines for a Thirtieth Birthday

Adoptees do not have the luxury of envisioning their celebrated births . . .
they often know nothing of their debuts . . .
JAN L. WALDRON, Giving Away Simone

You say you can't sleep nights, imagining them,
    the wayward girls of Omaha, Nebraska, 1965,
the chill green rooms of Booth Charity Hospital, bare
    as cloister cells, where they'll labor hard—*learn*

their lesson, the doctor says—and leave the infants
    they may name but not hold. It's the weekly outing
that gets you. Movies the Junior League springs for,
    something sweet at Dairy Queen, how, docile

as calves, they're led, in line, by twos, a few holding
    hands, like the schoolgirls they are. But look—here's
your mother, the copper hair she'll pass to you
    mirroring the late September sun, that same glamour-

puss mole etched on the still soft curve of her cheek.
    She won't line up, doesn't want ice cream, waits
outside, slouched against a red Mustang she'd like
    to own, smoking the Old Golds she knows say

bad girl, even now. Along the empty street,
    this part of town where no one comes, the first leaves
drop to skitter along the gutter, make her think
    of snow, the movie they've just seen—Lean's

Zhivago and Lara warm with vodka and lovemaking
    in a glistening blizzard of a house, snow veiling everything,
the gas lamps and satin couches, even the poet's desk
    slick with frost, of their lost daughter, how years

later, she refuses the proffered gift of her past.
    No Slavic romance in your mother's past,
just some west Nebraska town so small it's no more
    than a stutter in the long silence of the prairie,

her father's strap, regular as church once she began
    to show, the pursed mouth of her mother, a Greyhound
into this dirty city, where for days she slept and read
    from a book of names, choosing *Helen* for you,

maybe thinking of those thousand ships, maybe
    of some favorite teacher, one who called her writing
good. You can't know any of this, anymore than she knows
    it's just hours from your birth. I like to think you'll arrive

through a shared dream of iced and glittering Russian
    trees, Yuri smiling at the first sun he's seen in months
before turning to his work, that you debut to a welcoming
    chorus of *troika* bells and *balalaikas*, a cry of wolves.

for ECB

Anniversary

Somewhere between your mouth and my knees
the radio switches from Coltrane

       to Mozart and through the headboard
we can hear your parents thrashing.

We stiffen. I wonder about the rain
threatening the attic, your mother's hair swept

back, and when you raise yourself
over me, I close my eyes, imagine it streaming

over musty steamer trunks, the rusted spokes
of trikes, swamping your ancient

Southern Pacific, its shroud of webs
and long-abandoned yards

of figure-eight track. You whisper a story
about your last marriage, the dog

you owned named *Gringa*, how love
made her crazy and anything that moved, she'd attack:

the curtain beside your bed, your eyes.
Slipping a pillow under, you claim your father

had to put her down with a deer rifle.
Your mother laughs as I fit my hands to the small

of your back, your father's cry clears
the darkening rafters, and we begin to move.

Cleaning the Bank

A.J. dances the industrial-
sized vacuum around the locked and shining

desks, while our baby presses
half-circles of sweet oil from his palms

onto the beveled glass door.
I swipe, over and over, at the impossible

streaks on the other side,
the soft chamois damp in my hand,

the high-pitched smell
of ammonia raking my throat.

Invisible night-comers,
we empty mounds of lipsticked

butts into tin pails
and black plastic, stale smoke

and flurries of dust and ash
shrouding our clothes

and hair. And it doesn't matter
that it's dirty work, or

that years from now this moment
will crumble to shabby

nostalgia; that we'll divorce,
our child drift, unmoored, through changing

seasons, until he's distant
as these tellers and customers

we never see. For now, we're
almost happy, Velvet Underground

blaring from our almost-paid-for
jambox. We're singing

along, anarchist rock and roll
lyrics echoing off the vault's cool steel.

Nights Mutable as Water Revise
Themselves into the Shape of Our Extravagant Past

so that even the mildest gesture
astonishes, just as this night's fickle
snowfall startles the ripening orchard,

throngs of Cortland dwarfs, rimed
in silver, curving their slim branches
to dark earth. Trailing our rockiest

good intentions, that slipshod
cortège of poor elections and risky
marriages, we hurtled, breakneck,

toward a future dubious as any history
text. And maybe we were liars,
crooning blue lullabies as we battled

for purchase, ambitious for anything
costly, even these small, moony apples —
charming, but wrong.

Sonnet

after Robert Pinsky

Unwelcome April snow
shrouds the trees, just-greening
lawns. Landlocked rows

of unshuttered houses. Upstairs,
the mother falls through dreams
she won't remember, unaware

of wind troubling ice-etched
glass, her son, awake, imagining
a cool and final drift —

snow dry as gunpowder —
the easy float out of his skin.
He'll trace his name on the window,

then close his hands on silence,
the moon's invisible eye.

Sometimes When You're Asleep

and I'm counting the regular pulse
of the motel sign, its hothouse-
     flower vermilion splashed
on the musky rug, I remember the man

and woman I watched walking
     together under cottonwoods tall
and thick around as ancient
     columns, not touching, the absence
of touch somehow palpable

between them, I thought.
     It was one of those April days so blue
the sky seems lacquered,
     and I could hear jays and music
drifting past from the transistor radios

of children playing hooky.
     I thought they were probably in love,
though he was much younger,
     and only she wore a ring. I want
to wake you when I remember

how they stopped on a slight
     rise to watch as two gray-winged hawks
described an ellipse above the top
     branches, their paths cutting
across the sun. To ask if you believe,

as I do, that as they stood
     there, the woman squinting beneath
a shielding hand, the man's
     eyes behind dark glasses, the radiant
warmth of afternoon through their light

jackets, that it must have
   been for them a moment that even now
they remember, one of those days
   when you want so much you want nothing,
and everything isn't enough.

What It Is

Absent—that was what he was: so absent from everything most densely
real and near to those about him that it sometimes startled him to find
they still imagined he was there.
EDITH WHARTON, Age of Innocence

All morning the wind suggests
departure, troubling
the glass, ferrying the dead

leaves, lavish in their traveling
colors, from branch to gutter
as it makes for distant latitudes.

And it's erotic, isn't it—
the way it shifts, fickle, hushed
as an insinuating gesture,

among the lightening trees?
Maybe it's this novel I've been reading,
Wharton's Archer so *absent*

he's like a newborn, astonished
by anything—light sparking
off cut crystal, the cool timbre

of a woman's low voice.
And I must admit it scares me
to know so well those shadow

rooms he's cluttered with imaginary
furniture, what it is to bring
to them his cherished books

and company, to wait with him,
beneath a Paris sky the bluest
glacier could get lost in, losing

my place to this insistent wind,
until dusk, evening's resplendent pardon.

Twenty-five Years from Anywhere Like That

Shoulder, hip, and heel, I sprint
faster in my wingless Nikes, circling the Boys Town
track as Bonnie Raitt's roadhouse wail
and slide guitar snake wire.

Cottonwoods blur like a hypnotist's
watch until the track disappears and I'm back
in the third row of the Fillmore East,
where Janis Joplin, too wasted

to sing, slugged honeyed mash
from a high-tipped bottle. We sang "Ball and Chain"
a cappella on the D train, grinding
high notes breaking the national anthem

as the subway rocked the sour dark,
red and blue lights strobing.
That year, we traded up to barefoot rides
in limousines, four-way sunshine

for breakfast: onion grass
looney-tuning into little green men.
Now teenage girls from Boys Town pass me
quick, a middle-aged woman

they can't imagine seventeen, running away,
that burnt-out place
on Rickard Street, a bare mattress under
the corona of shotgun holes

left there for the landlord
by a flute player who cared for no one,
but sent his clear notes
up the fire escape, anyway.

III

Half-Light: No Feeling

And then winter, chill light
fading with the afternoon, the various grays
deepening to violet and charcoal
beyond the steam-clouded pane.
Her tea cooling in a chipped, enameled mug,

a young woman sits listening
to the voice of a man she once loved
swearing grief's whitened his hair
in the year since she left him, that he longs
for their child. The first streetlights

hum on and all along the block,
the tranquil glow of shuttered houses
in their yellow hoops of porch light,
as if nothing within could ever be too wrong.
Now the man weeps, he wants her to come

someplace he calls home, but she wants
only to forget him, which is why
she has traveled so far, leaving miles
of prairie and complicated highways,
the endless small towns, and filthy, dazzling

cities, those hundreds of thousands
of strangers, between them. I was that woman,
and nights like this, blues on the radio
and ice stippling every window, I try
to understand what love is, how it disappears

and leaves us strange to those once
ached for. Only images return: a flowered
cup on a sill, the early December dark.
A once-cherished voice, grown distant
as the moon. No feeling I can begin to name.

Winter Photograph of Brighton Beach, Brooklyn

Let's forget ex-husbands,
those lovers, that easy nostalgia—

radio oldies lulling
us to reverie, sorrow rising, luxuriant,

with the steam from our cups.

I'm tired of talk
about love. I want a clean mile

of sand around me,
the echo of boot heels on wood plank.

Salt in the wind.

The old women on the boardwalk
curl into the coats

and scarves of their Russian girlhoods.
Backs to the camera,

they squint toward Europe.

Ask them about love.
If I could, I'd step into this photo,

some steely Alice,
a Twilight Zone traveler. I'd stand

at the railing, my mind empty

as certain winter skies,
plumbing the fierce Atlantic cold,

the skitter and dive of fish.

Flying West

1

Lifting off from Kennedy,
swaddled in this mist's fine scrim,
my plane banks east
over darkening slabs and ledges,
slick basalt, the icy,
brackish waters of my childhood.
The moon's a flat wafer
signaling *slow* as we circle
west for Wright's Ohio.

2

Beneath the river continuously
losing itself, engulfed
somewhere I can't see by this vast,
salty surge, the graffiti-
less cars of the '65 IRT still bear
my sad father back from the City,
its glamour fallen from him,
shaken dust. He's reading
the *Post* — *Giants 24, Packers 17* —
one arm rocking gently
in the traction of a frayed strap.
He's slender as a boy.
The day's scheme of circles
and lines not yet permanently carved
on his face.

3

I try to sleep, call up
from the ocher light pooling
on my companion's novel
our kitchen's winter yellow, my mother
humming over fried potatoes,

cracked Melmac the color
of some nauseous sea, dime-store
glasses set for four.
The Edge of Night sends its strings
and quarrels across the hall.
Is she thinking of the sketch
she's left half-finished,
a hasty charcoal rose?

In the Frame

after Edward Hopper

Instead of the blonde, I'd paint my mother.
The sunlit dress can stay. Her hat and shadow
mean she's growing impatient,
and though her face says nothing, I know my
father's putting everything down
on a long shot, late.

I'd keep the limestone facade
behind her, the amber-lit hall, where my grandmother
pushes her janitor's mop and pail
along the staircase, her hands reddening
in ammonia. The blowsy
curtain marks my mother's bedroom,
bare dresser and narrow bed.

Younger than I am now, she can't
know the years of seasonal migrations, a wingless
bird behind the tinted windshield,
following horse trailers between Aqueduct
and Hialeah. She'll wait for hours
in the stark light of Hopper's summer evening,
and even if I wanted to, I couldn't
paint her rising.

Triptych: For Michael

My brother wakes at forty
on a solitary couch, slipped from comfort,

night's black shawl, his wife
and child adrift in rooms beyond

him, remote as stars
in the separate constellations

of their sleep. He's dreamed himself
as ravenous ghost, rises

to work—a self-portrait, the life-
sized cropping of his head doubled

on two panels. Such an intricate
and fraught choreography

as he pours the heated wax, its gold
fire veiling the image,

the image fading, a thickening
shroud obscuring, not quite revealing,

the other he seeks—and now the spilled wax—
his timing, for a moment, off—

its livid glove fused to his naked
hand. He must hold it, radiant with pain,

all night out the window, twelve
stories above Manhattan,

a small nova releasing
its human heat into the city's chill air.

* * *

Even as a child he sought
the fishable spot, a sleepwalker's faith
in the invisible drawing him

through the fertile dark
of our apartment, past the fixed
pole of our dreaming parents,

and once, out to the moon-soaked
street, so that, always, after,
the doors were double-locked.

I'd wake to fevered whispers,
him telling the beads of whatever vision
he'd shaped from the day, one arm

raised, a small divining rod,
as if already he knew a stream of secrets
roiled beneath us, dopplegängers

twinned our smiling, daylight selves.

* * *

Bee-spun yellow alchemized to savage
    red, black-hole black, the queasy green of decay
or money — *painting's like sex,*
    he says, at twenty means falls of molten wax

melded to six-foot swastikas, crosses,
    gritty punk stars he's layered to resemble
human flesh, reptilian skin, ocean, sky.
    Now it's faces and bodies that arrest

him, human icons the objects he must return
    to. He weds to them their second,
muslin skins, until they're shadow and question
    beneath wax cauls, luminous and mute

as angels are, as Michael, for a moment,
    is — see how he's held in the forgiving
half-light of the studio's oily haze,
    their messenger, object of their calm regard.

Grand Street

What if one Sunday morning on the Lower East Side
Christmas shoppers from Scarsdale
bundled in mink, their mouths bright with lipstick,
swirled, chattering like children
released from school, on their way to bargains
and light lunches, up the steep concrete
entrance to the IND, past a woman swaying
barefoot on the top step, wayward hair
swinging over her closed eyes as she rocked
precariously backward, her ribs
and cold-hardened nipples showing through a thin
nylon wrap, wailing, mournful as a bird,
a man's name you think may be *B-o-b-b-b-y, B-o-b-b-b-y,*
her speech too slurred for you to be sure?
What if your friend, no tourist like you, steered
you by one elbow through the perfumed air
trailed by the shoppers, saying *nothing we can do,*
she'd probably spit in our faces? Would you
imagine you knew the lives of those women,
console yourself with clichés of Valium
and infidelities, discontented sons and daughters
like your friend, and you, and maybe (thinking
you'd discovered some irony) like the woman
parting them easily as a traffic cop,
so gone she's left all of you invisible?
Wouldn't you still exclaim over mushroom loaf
and mashed potatoes at the famous dairy restaurant,
laughing at the comic waiters, their accents
like your grandfather's as they tell you
what to order? What if your friend pointed
out the beauty of the young girl working
the register, how she resembled a green-eyed,
bored madonna, handling the keys
and customers to the same, narcotic rhythm

as the woman keening on the subway steps, the traffic
cop rocking on his heels at the intersection,
holding herself the way the shoppers will hold their bags
all the way to Scarsdale, the way you
will hold your friend's arm as you walk back
past the IND, where no one will be
crying for Bobby; wouldn't you agree, saying,
Yes, she is a beauty, I can see that, yes?

SUSAN AIZENBERG

L'Heure Bleue

Pigeons furl the silk of their oilslick
    wings and doze on the limed shoulders
      of forgotten generals, while the last

commuters descend to the subways,
    where they'll sway above their papers,
      reflections streaming through the rapid

dark. Christened *bleue* by the French,
    this is the hour when evening raises
      its azure wand and the light smolders,

cool center of a candle flame,
    the five ring on an archer's target,
      a few stars the silvery nibs of arrows

just breaking through. Slender boys
    in waiters' tuxes snap starched linens
      over tables for two, as cabbies scour

backseats clean of the day's real
    detritus, and one by one, all over
      the city, vapor lamps spread their sodium

veils like some fast-traveling rumor,
    gild the drowsing streets, graffitied
      buildings, until even the harbor, the river

freighted with sludge, even the smoke-
    stacks percolating a foul snow of ash
      and grit over the Jersey Palisades,

have gone soft-focus, the whole town
    a Chamber of Commerce photo, or moony
      perfume ad. Prelude to the strict black

47

of night, this is the moment we may
    imagine the hiss of nylon, the garter
        a woman slides, high on her leg,

for a man dressing, even now, in his best
    suit, when we find ourselves humming
        Gershwin tunes, thinking *romance,*

possibility — of glamour we know better
    than by day. Which is why the woman
        lingers, her heart beating like a bird's

does, too quickly, why the man hesitates
    beneath her window, his face *chiaroscuro*
        in blue shadow, a square of light.

Paradise

This day, this turquoise

and green sunlit park, may be
romantic, but the diamond's

sculpted from rye grass,

where on a sandy mound
my young son winds up, lifts

his knee and sails the ball —

and yes, it trails a graceful arc

behind, connects with a smack, solid
in the catcher's oiled mitt. This day,

this day fevers the blood, until past lives fade in —

those autumn nights when cool dark pastures
were oceans we swam,

flannel-shirted, barefoot, buoyed

by jug wine and mescaline, either shore

a paradise of orchards, apples
fragant, so heavy on the silvered trees,

shimmering past lives

we can't talk about,
    gone, and so immutable —

             want out, and wildly our hearts
        knock in their cages,

                    yes, like birds craving the air.

Mark Turpin
Nailer

MARK TURPIN's poems have appeared in journals including the *Paris Review*, *Ploughshares*, the *Boston Review*, and the *Threepenny Review*. He is presently at work as a master carpenter rebuilding a house in the Oakland / Berkeley hills, site of the 1991 firestorm, where he has practiced his trade for twenty years.

To R

The Box

When I see driven nails I think of the hammer and the hand,
his mood, the weather, the time of year, what he packed
for lunch, how built-up was the house,
the neighborhood, could he see another job from here?

And where was the lumber stacked, in what closet
stood the nail kegs, where did the boss unroll
the plans, which room was chosen for lunch? And where
did the sun strike first? Which wall cut the wind?

What was the picture in his mind as the hammer
hit the nail? A conversation? Another joke, a cigarette
or Friday, getting drunk, a woman, his wife, his youngest
kid or a side job he planned to make ends meet?

Maybe he pictured just the nail,
the slight swirl in the center of the head and raised
the hammer, and brought it down with fury and with skill
and sank it with a single blow.

Not a difficult trick for a journeyman, no harder
than figuring stairs or a hip-and-valley roof
or staking out a lot, but neither is a house,
a house is just a box fastened with thousands of nails.

Pickwork

There is skill to it, how you hold your back all day, the dole
of force behind the stroke, the size of bite, where
to hit, and knowing behind each swing a thousand others wait
in an eight-hour day.

And if the head suddenly comes rattling down the handle:
knowing to drive a nail for a wedge between the wood and the steel.
The inexperienced pretend to see in the dirt a face they hate,
and exhaust themselves. The best

measure themselves against an arbitrary goal, this much
before lunch, before break, before a drink of water, and then
do it. Some listen to the pleasant ringing
of the pick, or music, and trancelike, follow the rhythm

of the swing. Once I spent a half hour attentive
only to my muscles triggering into motion, sweat
creeping down my chest. Ground makes the biggest difference.
In sandstone you feel the impact to your knees,

in mud you yank the point from the muck each throw.
The hardest part is not to let the rhythm fail,
like stopping too often to remeasure the depth, stalling
in the shithouse, losing self-respect, or beginning to doubt:

Am I cutting too wide? Is the line still straight?
Or thinking of backhoes, more help, quibbling inches
with the boss. On my job Lorenzo works in the sun all day,
his silver radio quietly tuned to the Mexican station.

Shoveling out, he shrugs and says, "No problem, Mark,"
waist-deep in the hole.
From the spot I work, I hear the strike of his pick all day.
Driving home together he has told me about his two black whores,

his ex and daughter in L.A., and Susan Nero, "on-stage." Thirteen times
he's seen her. Almost reverent, he says, "She is so beautiful,"
and makes immense cups with his hands.
And driving home he has told me of his landlord who extorts him

for the green card he doesn't have, of his "mo-ther"
dying of cancer in Mexico City, of his son-of-a-bitch
dad who beat him, and her, and ran away, of his brother Michael,
and Joaquim, in Chicago, the central valley. In the car

he asks me if I think the boss will hold half his pay, he needs
to save something for his sister
—I hear his pick all day
and in the afternoon I go out to ask him, how's it going?

He shrugs me off. "It's no big problem, Mark.
No problem, I can do it, but the fucking pick is dull,"
and shows me the blunted steel point. "I need something—
sharper, you know: I need a sharper pick."

Last Hired

On Monday returned the man I fired
wanting the phone number of the laborer he loaned money to,
and stood while I wrote it out on a scrap of shingle
and the crew on the floor kept hammering

with the silence of three hammers tapping out different beats.
I scratched down the name and seven digits with a flat pencil
scrawling across the ridged grain and then with it.
He thanked me with an uncomfortable smile and left.

He was incompetent, but incompetence is not a crime
—I never liked him.
Out of almost pure intuition, right from the beginning
and I noticed how quickly the other men closed in beside me

against him. He must have felt it, too,
those days as he knocked the nails out of his screwed-up formwork,
and spit saliva in the hammermarks of his windowsills
to raise the grain. Must have every day

felt more alone. He had a habit of mumbling explanations
that trailed into incoherence. But he was not a stupid man.
When I asked him to repeat himself, he shrugged me off
with a sigh and asked me what I wanted him to do.

The morning I fired him I walked down to the street
before he could leave his truck, and was on the way surprised
and annoyed by a hypocritical watering in my eyes that went away.
Then catching him, saw-in-hand, I told him to go back to the truck.

I said it deliberately hard, so he would guess
before I said the words. Then we stood together. And he took it
as if he expected, and failure were something he had grown around.
Then he got in his truck, drove the street, and was gone.

Photograph from Antietam

"Dead Confederate Soldier"

GARDNER, CATALOG #554

Around him is battlefield litter,
dew-swollen lumps of a spilled powder. What is it?
And the strips of cloth. Left behind
the lines of men that advanced or fell farther on

or hid somehow on this trampled field
of Maryland grass. By chance, at the extreme upper
edge of the photo—"unmistakable, but barely discernible
in the distance"—soldiers dragged into a long row,

their uniforms, the dark Union "Shoddy" or Confederate gray
and the white? The white hairy stomach and thigh of a Union man,
whose trousers were left undone
by soldiers who looked at the wound and crawled off

—hardly more than unfocused grayscale. But here on the ground
photographed is one dead: sharp as a flower
and sprawled in the posture of ease,
one bent arm behind his head.

From the waist down it is hard to tell
his legs from bedding, his form is lost in rags,
his chest protrudes contortedly from a nest of rags.
Both sleeves are rolled, and a vein

in the crooked forearm still seems to bulge—
the other lies on his chest, pale and marble, feminine,
hand hidden at the wrist.
From the nose and eye, two dried black tears

of blood streak his cheek and forehead.
On his chin: two tufts of a cleft goatee, a devil's beard
—maybe he was a devil—he seems so young,
tossed and wrecked by the war.

In the zone of sharpness and contrast around his form
the blades of grass and sticks
seem to turn around him, the configuration of each twig
and clump of moss

quite apparent, yet abstracted into a circle
of random and spiked white signs
floating around him in nature's meaningless codes
for mishap or premature death.

You can see he lies in the shallowest of crevices,
not man-dug—as if pubes of the earth were
already forming up and around, drawing him back in—
a pitiful breastworks.

Likely it was only a spot where he had chosen to fire temporarily,
crossing this field. Or a friend pulled him here dying,
or he came to it himself during the battle
to prevent being wounded again.

Shithouse

Illiterate, banal, scrawled in ink, fingered in shit,
even blood—or penciled painstakingly
until lead clung to the letters ploughed

into the plastic wall;
some messages so impersonal they surprise by the need
to be said at all: Fuck.

Others are illumined with autonomous cocks and balls,
spread female legs like wings
with the cunt scratched furiously.

One I saw, a squirrel, his face void of expression
except intentness, licking
his own huge human-sized dick and balls—as if cracking a nut,

the four black marking-penned
spurts of cum, in parody of tears, falling from it;
the figure obviously worked on

to get it right:
forearms like crazed wires where he labored
frustrated to fix how they cross the torso,

the tiny strokes of scrotum hairs
coaxed from the blunt black pen, the gratuitous branch—
as if loathing were art. As if it weren't.

Carpenter

Unasked, he once said what he required of life
and I was more surprised by the occasion of his
telling me than by his simple words:
rest when he got home, beer, and sports on TV;

he said it earnestly without swagger or resignation,
with the pride and appraisal of a man who perceived
himself ordinary and wanted what he had.
And I wondered if his flatness was meant to be

a check to me, carpenter, same as him but with desires
flagrant and helplessly exposed by the years.
He held the rope while I drove nails
at the edge of a steep roof above a 60-foot drop.

I trusted him not because he was the least imaginative
but because he understood and accepted that I was scared.
A kind of respect really. As much as I longed
to tell my secrets he kept his mostly,

sitting on the ridge awkwardly transferring
a cigarette from hand to lip
as he adjusted the rope around his back and down to me—
occasionally holding it with one hand

as he took a drag, though not thoughtlessly.
He tied steel his first day, an apprentice
from the union accustomed to abuse, his hands clumsy
with the linesman's pliers but fast

from effort instead of skill—the sharp wire
leaving a dozen marks of his work
on the back of his hands before lunch.
In the union he only learned to run shearwall,

miles of it, but these mornings walking with cigarette
and coffee from his truck he asks about the day:
"What's up?" regarding me on his heels,
having learned most of what I've taught.

Now with a family at thirty-four his belly sags,
and when he runs the bases he comes back to the bench
with pain in his chest. On the phone his wife tells me
of him standing in her kitchen, tool belt on,

with the six-foot level I gave him for his birthday,
saying "Hey Hon, look!" And on the jobsite
we crown and cut a beam that we will raise to span
two gables and support the rafters on the roof

while discussing how to set the ladders, and who gets which
end: getting tasks and calls straight—then leaning, reaching
from his ladder, guiding the beam to the wall he grins
at me grimacing, anticipates the weight.

Will Turpin b. 1987

The eyes are slits—the pupils grayest blue.
The eyebrows: two watercolor lines,
brush dipped only in water. On the nose's tip

is a minute field of white pimples . . .
Sucking so far is what he does best,
pulling with short intent strokes, or recklessly

(for the pleasure of recklessness it seems)
releasing the rubber nipple almost to the tip
then sucking in hard.

When it drops out he cries, feels the brush
of lips across his face, cooing; then pacified,
sucks again, follows motion with his eyes.

Laborer's Code

A plot plan tells a history of a lot before a job,
the surveyor's name and number, year he drove his stakes
and set sea-level elevations of hubs and monuments

—but the laborer has never seen it. He doesn't give a shit,
piecemeal is his stock-in-trade: to this depth
the ground is razed and that—the string stretched there—

is the property line, sagging across the view.
Sunlight bears on the stack of studs where lunch hour goes
in an arc of exhausted silence. He rips a bag of chips,

pops a coke. The front page is news; he talks
fishing trip, violence, checks, half-aware he's said
it all before—what more can he say?

When it's time, he stands and throws
mere fill-in shovelwidths somewhere over his left shoulder
for the pleasure of shoving the shovel in.

Downslope

From a point across, the lot seemed floating down on seas
Of poison oak, hung on the hillside
As if on the back of a monstrous wave—
And spotting the long slope were shadows of scrub pine
In the heat and Sticky Monkey Bush
    And the lot was a bare field of plywood covers

Staked and sealed with mud, protecting the drilled holes.
Winched-down creaking
On the one-inch cable its grunting tonnage hung from,
The driller's *CAT* wore a groove in the road
And rutted the asphalt berm on the shoulder of the road
    Where the cable crossed to the *deadman*

That twisted and ovaled the hole it stood in
With the weight. Cuts two feet deep
Marked the slope where he spun a track, and the topsoil
And scree flung from the spinning drill
Was loose and drifted downhill in fanning alluvial flows
    —The workmen lost pocket tools half-climbing,

Half-sliding down. The operator's helper, when the auger
Surfaced from a hole, signed him to stop
With a finger pointed to a tooth, then unwedged
The resinous roots from the cutting teeth. Across the slope,
The plain stripped twigs of it, coated with dust
    Still stayed nearly upright and oozed

The harmlessly poisonous, telltale black sap.
Mindless, the operator's helper yanked a bulbous
Blackened root as thick as a thumb
And pantomimed: thrusting and stirring its length
In a cunt in the air while the operator grinned.
    Then he bent to stroke a fingermark in the hydraulic grease

Flowing down the Kelly bar, as the auger disappeared
In the sandstone—the spirals
Of its turns, carved and smoking on the sides of the hole.
Standing beside them in the equipment's roar
Momentarily I felt afraid of falling in headfirst,
    Of struggling

Toward a spot of light above my feet,
When the operator inadvertently hooked a waist-high boulder
That burst from the ground clad in dirt, raw with the veins
Of roots, loose flakes; and he tried, wildly flipping
The yellow, loose-jointed controls to ease it onto
    The edge of the CAT's blade while his man

Cursed, and shoved ineffectually, watching for his fingers
As the steel groaned, scoring a gray scar
On the wobbling stone. And then this memory: The stone,
As it casually rolled free—and the operator's helper,
Arms in the air, chasing it with feet pounding: running
    Madly down the grade.

Foundation

Slipping
clods, rolling
particles of
rock and mud:

what was shoveled
out down the
slope flowed
like lava over

their boot tops,
and filled each
tread that pressed
the sliding earth

to itself because
it was what
was solid and
bore their feet.

Hammer

Head-heavy, hickory worn
to a walnut color,
you get to know its feel,
how the ripping-claw curves
and tapers to a chisel edge,
the rising tone of the nail
till it sinks and the hammer thuds.

Or pulling it up suddenly
off a nailhead like a button—
letting it ring in the air.
Gene Lance showed me how
to never miss and kept fingers
pinched around the nail
as he drove it in.

Hands and fingers: ten-odd
cuts, blisters, splinters,
none bad enough to pull,
the smooth crescent bulge
of a fingernail growing back in,
a framing callus. Missing once
I blackened my eye knocking

off a brace, and once took
a splinter the size of a pencil
beneath the vein in my right arm.
The carpenter Chris fired,
he felt the hammer his last day,
raising a big wall that broke free
and collapsed, all of us getting

away but him, left crumpled
and pinned beneath the studs,

the wall bearing on his collarbone,
his cocaine habit, divorce, $50,000 debt
to the rehabilitation clinic (Chris
said he was just tired of hearing him
say cunt all day)—dragged

convulsive across the floor, the builder's
wife posed beside his head, sunlight
harsh across the plywood floor
except for the shade his body made—
and Chris, guilty, blind, hectoring,
hammer-in-hand, lining the men up
to raise the wall again.

Before Groundbreak

Off work and going upslope for a look
I left the plans, to see the view
Their money bought, weighted with a rock,

And trampled a path of parted weeds
Past pampas, nettles,
Poison oak bristling in the breeze,

A weathered 2x4 nailed high up in a cedar's fork,
A haggard pair of panties waving stiffly from a thorn—
I walked where they would walk.

Standing there, out of breath, where
They would soon stand, vacuuming
Or reaching for a towel—how bare

And graspable it will seem,
And ever-present, our time and effort spent.

Aubade

Because of the enormous trees standing just outside,
dawn won't reach their bedroom windows for hours,
though already a jay cackles and flashes past,

each mullioned pane framing a blur of blue.
Strangely awake, he watches this, and talks
to her, though she is asleep, wants and needs

to sleep, but answers him sweetly with a little girl's
voice that seemed to him so uncharacteristic when
they were first together. Sitting up, he is naked

under the covers. And asleep next to him, she is naked
under the covers. Though not keenly amorous, he hooks
his knee over her hip, and pets her, and she arches

under his hand. And though not feeling particularly
loving and in fact, thinking of it as a little cruel,
he whispers he loves her into her ear, enjoying

her pleasure at it. He does love her.
And he strokes her again, though this touch undoes
the others, tells her to go to sleep.

Also cruel, he thinks, and watches
the feeding jay turn, pump his winged shoulders twice
and disappear into the oak tree.

Raising Walls

Frame of a house in the sun
Against the sky.
Honeybees buzzing between the rafters,
Noon voices buzzing below the rafters.

The urge always upwards—joist, stud,
Rafter, ridge.
Arches and portals;
Ribs of whales and elephants.

Nailer

Although it is a Sunday
across a cleared tract
of mud and standing water about the space of Disneyland
where dots of birds pick singly
and huge yellow *CATs* and backhoes wait in Titan postures—
a carpenter, a pieceworker
is nailing on the solitary gray square of a new foundation,
flopping the plywood sheets down on the joists,
his hammer winking across the mud brown expanse
and music from a parked pickup,
no walls yet, more like a dance floor than a house.
Bent down on his knees,
watching his hands work upon the plywood deck marked with
driven shining heads, he plays a game of thinking
separate thoughts, but drifts . . . the unbuttoned edges
of his workshirt swaying, right arm in a whipping motion,
left hand fat with nails.
By feel he turns the heads up, points down for the set and imagines
each brute particular fastened by a nail: one nail
for a puff of cloud, one for the shadowed hill,
one nail for the red tail on the ridge, one nail
for his pickup . . . one and one and one . . .
"six inches on center on the edges, twelve in the field"
—the floor honey like a field
but close-up, the grains run in exotic swirls
of rust and tan and chocolate brown, bits of cedar green, eddies
of blue, and gray when a sheet was used to cover a stack,
all between his knees, rippling, flaming
stitched in spots where the wood is weak, flowing
into pulses of black knots or flatter grains,
chunks of bark, mildew, delicate green scums . . . Sidling
on the floor, the denim of both knees worn completely through,
he daydreams on a sea of nailheads flashing
like wavetips . . . one and one and one and one . . .

But all around him are puddles the length of football fields
reflecting the sky in shapes
and gouged up through are the roots of trees,
balled-up wire fencing, buckets, fifty-gallon drums: debris,
and mounds bulldozed up
and ranged along the borders of the tract, embedded
with jagged chunks of concrete slab, galvanized
pipe bent oddly, stones the size of duffel bags
—here and there are smaller piles of concrete rubble heaped up—
to be hauled away? Or spread for fill?
A home owner might find a buried layer beneath the soil in his yard.
Cement and sand and gravel, concrete
is what the world is built of, gushes rattling into
roads and dams, bears the iron of bridges in bay mud.
Green, it is as brittle as chalk
and warm to the touch. Two hundred years: it rots like wood.
In 28 days the test cylinder of a 7-sack mix
is hard like real rock.
To the west, a monster storm pool reaches toward the road,
its surface silver, or steel,
the color of skyscrapers, steel. A man-high lumber stack leans
skirted in mud—the lowest studs completely sunk.
And the heavy equipment too is splattered over nicked and scratched
yellow paint—and their tracks and wheels and underpinnings,
the welded steel teeth and nuts as big as fists
are smeared and caked with clods and grass, their buckets
half-full of rainwater. Even the street ending
at the guardrail is brown, and at the intersection
a thousand muddy stripes shoot out.

I have worked on a similar, smaller job—
in the rain with two others, hauled a mud-slippery
concrete-shooting pumphose in hectic, sloppy efforts over
form walls, through boot-high water, first sliding, then falling,
trying to get the thing to budge, then, to get a grip,
the mix first clumping out like turds,

then arching into a stream, pushing the lead man back, his boots
slipping on the mud. The operator holds the 4-inch squirting hose
to his genitals and calls it an "elephant's dick."
Two hundred feet long: six feet of it weigh a hundred pounds.

It is primordial, we serve it
banging on the forms to keep the concrete flowing, mud from it
on our hands, foreheads, noses, our clothes completely brown
even in our pockets—the driver
leaving the cab, walking to the hopper for a match as
rain showers on the pumper, the forms in the muddy field,
as the level in the forms rises
and the concrete begins to set.

In Winter

These days in winter when the weather breaks for a spell
I return to the job thinking about
children, money, and divorce—

and sweep sliding pools of sawdust and rainwater
off the bloated plywood floor.
The rooms: dripping, dark—

smell of cigarette smoke, fir, and wool
as men splash from room to room in rubber boots and slickers,
nailing up the power cords from the water.

I'm amazed I'm here sometimes, doing this work with these men,
and sometimes expect them to find me out—though they never act
as if I am not where I am supposed to be.

They smile and joke with me, respect me.
Outside the frame of a window I see stumps of three plum trees
that yesterday we cut down with a chain saw—

and where the branches fell into puddles among the hillocks
of mud the water is stained a wine red—
and a shower of pale pink petals rings the dumpster.

When I lived with her, I never thought about my daughter
during the day, while I worked, while she sat in school
among strangers' children. Or if I did

it was with a kind of mustered poignance—
she would be there when I got home. But now, thinking of her,
I remember sitting in wooden chairs,

boredom, anxiety, and guilt swirling in my head,
what I was required to know but didn't
about Asia, mathematics, what someone said.

Muse

Once present in a sapless tailing of 2x4
As it fell from the saw,
In a hammer-bent nail, in the white unmuscled
Spine of a weekend laborer,
In winter sun. State of mind: Illusion,
Conviction, crass confidence.

Everything under the Sun

From the station platform you can see them, the rooftops
over East 14th at sundown, mostly above
the depressed corner markets, the broke beauty salons:
   King's and Queen's
Hair Throne—the sun sparking flecks of light

on the lakes of tar and gravel littered with glass fifths
and pint empties. Below, the drag slides through the rest
of East Oakland or drifts into quiet, working neighborhoods lodged
between darker blocks, flattops beside flattops shading

the blistered gables of asphalt shingles, sagging and spotted
with coldpatch—the streets lined with pickups and campervans,
   mild yards
in golden crosslight, burnt brown, overgrown,
with neat chain-link fences, plaster statuary, bare dirt rose gardens

—the hard city soil a stratum of antstakes and engine oil
beaten to a powdery dust. Along a concrete drive
five Cambodian men dig out their sewer, joking, tossing
cigarettes in the trench, and up a block in the last light

two carpenters work tearing off a roof, their spades
shining a dim pink, dipping into the black widening hole.
An old woman watches them from her yard and remembers two
   carpenters before the war
swinging lunch pails with linked arms

walking to the trolley, as the carpenters above rip
through the thick, desiccated buildup of courses buckled and frayed,
coming off in striated chunks of tar and wood, each failed
relic layer, struck with twenty years of sun, shingled over till

new nails wouldn't grab in the black, disintegrating
layer the first roofer split and laid—*the lowest is always cedar:*
making a dust like grease that halos your sweating skin,
blackens Kleenex at the sink—but the roofer's nose

was so used to the stink of cedar he said he couldn't smell it
and his scrawny back was reddish brown with the same rays of sun
that fell on her old carpenters, and shone on her husband's
    greased, jet hair:
now he sits on the couch at the living-room window,

washed in the light, contracted deep inside his disease;—
    and at a touch
shingles crumble and fall through the attic, and the mass
    on the roof ridge
slides to the gutter, spilling near the barrow where a laborer stands;
she squeezes his arm; *His last stroke I told the driver*

to turn off his damn siren until we were out of the neighborhood.
Along the ridge the two men move slowly, crab-wise, flattening
the hundreds of small rusted nails that protrude, as bits of tar paper fall,
looping toward the ground. At the roof edge: one of the two—

his shape, a black spot crawling across the sun.
From a back patio crowded with family a Mexican girl looks up
and stretches as she talks, feeling him look at her,
her bent wrists pressed to the small of her back, making chicken wings,

his attention drawing something out of her,
the way a boy's mouth drew blood through her skin and left the
    pink mark
she strokes absently, picturing herself
in the carpenter's eyes as he sends a dribble of roof dust

off the edge, a crown of sun above his head shining onto her skin,
    making her
feel weak, everything crisscrossing the world's face in giddy tides

as she hooks her toes on the bottom porch rail,
lying back, her little brothers skidding through the grass.

And across from them is a yard where a mason once stood,
    ball game on,
laboring on his own wall of brick with brick tracery and columns
    of brick,
talking with neighbors, the trowel clinking as he buttered one face
and one edge before laying a brick and trimming the mud, each joint

a sealed darkness beneath the crazed surface; the work
raising a course at a time on the quiet street—his patterns:
    herringbone,
fluted, and niched—each capital topped bizarrely with two bricks
leaning together, the upper, resting corners fast in a pinch of mortar.

Suzanne Qualls

Beauty, and Instinct

SUZANNE QUALLS was born in Stockton, California and attended UC Berkeley as an undergraduate and graduate student. Her poems and translations have appeared in a number of journals. She has performed "House of Wreckers," an autobiographical monologue, in New York and San Francisco.

for David Qualls

Au Pair

The crowds are delirious in the streets
of Baghdad. Another war has ended.
A general raises hands to his face,
vanquishing tears as he enters the mosque,
once at eight o'clock, again at midnight.
In the street, men weep and shout, and
raise their hands, tight-fisted. Women
in black are picking bodies from the rubble;
the living are unburied, weeping—
                                    and here,
having drunk too much, limbs loose and
desirous, I remember whispering in darkness,

and then the little girl I baby-sat: her mother
gone, afraid of sleep, she cried and struck
the door until I came to open it against
the gathered fury of her weight.
Walking back and forth until she quieted,
I laid her down to sleep; she cried again
and reached for me in the dark, to which
we had become accustomed.

                        Later, as I held
her hand and spoke to her continually,
keeping the tone, against my impulses,
gentle and low, I almost thought her gone.
But in the blackness, as I stirred to leave,
I saw her eyes opened wide and blank,
her being set apart, poorly comforted,
inconsolate, but tired—

                               I felt pity
rising in me for all the eyes opened into absence,
unlucky, condemned to puny chances

                          —then it seemed
to me that pity was false, mere solemnity,
an affectation, without value.

Laurie's Mother Back from the Dead

It might have been the change of seasons,
so subtle here in California they occur
unperceived by outsiders . . . or the failure
of rain and the vast false blooming of flowers
that caused her sleeplessness. Caused her
to wake me, every hour from three
until seven this morning. I even think
she may portend an earthquake. On your side
of the globe, only animals
are thought to know such things.

But I woke to hear your mother's voice condemning me:
"This is not what I have grown to expect;
you have cultivated my daughter's friendship,
now you are ignoring her.
Now she is on a strange continent, away
from my ashes that have been dispersed
by water and air, away from her father,
who still lives, plays tennis, learns to cook,
and worries. I, who was her bitter rival
in her home, I, who made her hazardous,
I made her conscious
of phone calls, letters, birthday presents, thank-you notes,
all the continuing forms of renewed obligation—
I have abandoned her to this world,
my own daughter, my thick-fisted baby, my prize.
You have broken the rules again.
She will be furious.

You do not understand what she requires.
Or worse—you fail to honor it.
Reverie, rumor, good intentions, are all lost
in the logic of expanding space.
Unarticulated devotion is no devotion

at all. I have taught her to require
the recurring gift.
My first husband was a nothing,
but I learned from him:
trust only coats, apartments, the things
in the hand, the *intended* child.
You who believe in the existence
of things that cannot be seen,
and who busy yourself naming them:
you have been unfaithful to my daughter."

So how do I explain it?
I can see, waking today, there is more
color in my face . . . and this morning
I was jubilant for a moment.

It might have been the clacking
of garbage cans or the hooting and
joking of the garbage men in the street;
or the thrill of that enormous truck
—once filled with the neighborhood's refuse,
it consumes, compacts, revises, and roars.

Encomium

People ask me how I am
and I begin to praise my cat.
When I come home, she always greets me.
She comes down the street
from the neighbor's yard
where she's been sleeping,
or if she's been
on the roof, she pokes her head
vertiginously over the edge,
and begins to complain
that I left her stranded.
She knows the sound of my car.
Even the neighbors have noticed.
The lawyer across the street remarked,
as she came mewing impatiently,
stopping to be petted,
allowing herself to be lifted
to my shoulder, then
carried to the door:
"She's very loyal."

I like that, the pleasure
in companionship, in falling
short of her expectations,
the reproach of an intimate
for some small domestic infraction —
the very expectations
themselves a kind of privilege,
the attendant pleasures of peace,
a luxury of pets.

Even my veterinarian knows,
without condescending,
that she is my family,

that she is exacting. She and I—
we suffer mutual indebtedness:
I enjoy her complaints;
she teaches contemplation.

She stops eating, walks
to a closed cabinet, effortlessly
opens the door with one paw, her life mask
of elaborate eye makeup,
Cleopatrine eyes and elegant whiskers
disappears, and all I can see
are her hind legs,
the legs of a dancer—always light,
the feet slightly splayed
from the hip, as she enters
the cabinet, curiously,
and with real interest
to see what she has seen
so many times before.

Places

Think about Collette, her shrinking—
she wrote about the paperweights around her bed.
David yesterday speaking of Rod. Sue asked him,
once he knew he was dying, what he wanted.
Take an ambulance back to Nevada City.
Look out the window.

David saying he had more choice than most, trying
to grant the guy a little will, it's not all bad.
Rod wanted to go back to Nevada City.
Two days contemplating the landscape.
And Joel in his living room in a hospital bed.
How important it became—
Joel was out in the back.
He sat on the patio yesterday.

I can't imagine that you look at things any harder.
I'm not even sure he saw much.
Where would I go? Back to this bed next to the windows
looking at the unrevised backyard, everything
I was dissatisfied with.
All the places we imagine ourselves to be. All the places we have been.
My backyard needs work. Everything emblematic.
Everything taking on poignancy, that is, forced
to stand in for everything else.
And doing it. Easily.

Ralegh's History of the World, an Epitaph for Bent

Plato's Longing was more decorous than mine —
difference marked the distance from fulfillment,
the measure of love was the depth of its incapacity

—no clowns like me ignoring the law
holding the gaze of a dying animal, likely
scaring her with my grief, saying
I love you, the chant over and over becoming a song
of helplessness across floating waters,
the tiny boat floating away on pure weakness,
caught in a placid tide; and I,
Picture of Sincerity, Body of Devotion
carried on.

Some would compare this grief to others
and find it slight among the world of cares
but I rebel against that measure
and seek a way to bring this heart to bear

—there was in you a consciousness of me,
your eyes sought mine so carefully,
and as you sank within the deepest of the seas
that I loved you and that you could love me
was simple.

Experience and Truth, twinned virtues, flank the bellied
breasted woman holding up the world, her head
surrounded by the shooting fires of the sun;
Good Fame and Bad Fame blow horns above a globe
whose botched continents show what we know by now —
Experience is sad, and Veritas is beautiful.

Old Story

The ancients who thought about love
      considered it
madness in which the soul
      loses possession
of itself. To Lucretius, love was
      a disease,
an aberration to be cured
      by philosophy.

When Achilles mourned Patroclus, he was
      inconsolable.
Thetis, his mother, told him: "Sleep
      with another,
even a woman. The gods are bored
      by your grief."

Then Patroclus came back from the dead.
      He said:
"Achilles, put my ashes
      in your urn,
and our limbs will twine eternally."

Achilles prepared for battle.

Early in a Rotten Summer

Early in a rotten summer
I got a cat. (Over your objections,
but what could *you* say about it.)
And then later you got a cat
of your own;
a tacit experiment with love
—independent responsibility
for independent beasts—
fishing for the hook
that's what we were doing.

You began to like my cat.
I remember you said exactly that.
"I like your kitty," you said.
And I thought
how pathetic the word "kitty" was,
that tenderness,
your sovereignty showing clearly.

And although I said I liked your cat,
that was not exactly the case.
She was too soft for my taste,
and too pretty.
She had not come to you,
forsaking all others, *out of will.*
She had been chosen, and looked it—
like a kitten on a calendar
like a birthday card from my grandmother.
Oh Christ, I thought when I saw her:
She is *easy* to love.

The Wrong Son

Stepping into the accumulated
impersonal heat of late afternoon
I imagine you in Los Angeles, standing
in your father's death room,
feeling like the wrong son.

"If you think he's good,"
he remarked at your graduation,
"you should meet my other son,"
—a day like this one, warm
air dense and still.

But you tell me most of that bravado
is gone now, and you stand next to a man
who is embarrassed by dying,
a stick with an angry stick
of an arm, trying to throw off

an oxygen mask:
"You don't see me like this," he whispers.
Turning into the driveway of a ranch-style house
its three garages at an angle to the street,
custom designed to include the particular

comforts of a particular life, you realize
that an education is beginning:
all your chances to change
or to make things different
narrow to the crest of a suburban block

and you notice, as you're thinking
This is the Big Time This only happens once
that the same light lacerating
your numb heart
has flushed all the houses on the street.

To a Young Man Who Wants to Return Early from a Trip

First of all, I love you.
But I'm not in love with you,
Nor do I hope to be.
Being in love cannot be calculated;
It takes you by surprise, and is unpleasant.
Someone said that to me, once.
I didn't like it.
You don't like it, either.
You probably also hate the part
About your youth. I can't do
Anything about that.

So I have begun all wrong—
That's established—
And you are homesick:
People are nice, but Europe
Is a disappointment. Things aren't
Different enough.

You imagine returning home.
That is, you imagine going back
To where you've been.
You will have friends there,
Favorite restaurants,
You will know the street names—
I'll be there. But things will
Be the same: I mean, things
Won't be different enough there, either.

If it is true that you will be
Returning home to me, I have to say
That would be a big mistake.
Things are the same here;
Nothing has changed; but I am

Quite different. I am not, after all,
Your home. And this is the sad part:
You don't have a home.
But you should take heart.
Don't be so discouraged—
It's a common problem.
Homes take you by surprise, too.
They take a long time, and like
Love, they're sometimes better lost.

This is not to say that you have
Lost me, or lost love, or lost a home.
I am here, love hangs somewhere
In the space between us, and home
Is elusive. It will be like this
Until you get back, and for a long time
After. So there is no need to hurry.
I wish for you to see things,
And not yearn so much.

Katie Can't Go Out Today

Today I wish that I could learn
some Eastern discipline,
exhaling all my need.
One needs, you know, (I do)—but need
becomes too large for our support:
I fear I'll need so much
I'll force myself to lose.

The little girl across the street
is angering her father:
"Okay, that's it," he says,
"forget it. You don't get to go."
I think she's learning what I'm learning—
something we don't want to know.

I listened to you speak
about the women you have loved,
the ones you've had and lost,
and had and lost again.
For a moment I grew silent,
sobered by the thought
your love had touched you deeply
more often than my own.

Who's counting? It's useless
to compare—and certain folly
to defend this course of thought.

But think I do, relentlessly
in fact, and self-indulge,
and wrack my brain,
and lose, and lose again.

The saints and sages knew the truth—
there's bliss in letting go.
Ah, bliss—now I remember it,
that's where the problem lies.
Remembering is bliss's curse:
it gives, and it denies.

Katie can't go out today,
she disobeyed her father.
She's crying, now—she really hurts—
it's obvious she cares.
She can't go out and pet the cat
that's lying on the stairs.
I'd like to go and comfort her,
and let her comfort me,
to share the stoop and tell her
that tomorrow she can go:

I'll stroke her hair and tell her
she's a pretty little girl.

Death of a Scholar

for J.F.

Insectoid, all instinct, his limbs drawn up
and atrophied, the body spindled, past
any moment of relaxation into the bed,
the bed permanently cranked up behind back
and knees—his olive skin, once famously soft
("I always thought he smelled like lemons," his first wife said)
now more olive, deeper into shades
of gray and brown, the color absolutely wrong.

All this and his sheets strung over him,
the angles of his limbs acute,
his drapery sometimes slipping
from a promontory, exposing all
luckless accidents: crisscrossed
abdominal scars, in varying degrees
of freshness, emitting fine clear plastic tubes;
everything permitted now, tolerated,
even the one infected scar
allowed to seep and redden, as the nurse, exasperated,
in tones fit for little boys too long
too quiet, and found to have misbehaved:
"There's nothing we can do for you. You're terminal."
But even she, the mythmakers now agree,
was finally brought round to "say hi"
through another nurse who helped you move
from hospital to home. This, we felt,
was testament of your worthiness;
we wanted to believe your suffering
had cracked the heart of someone for whom death
had lost all particularity;
a tired witness to our agonies

and transports, she had become
philosopher: she couldn't even see a point
in lessening your pain.

                    All angles now,
the skin too large, the heavy crest
of hair too fertile for what's left,
your head bent toward your chest, the dry
and wrinkling skin now more like hide—
but you, refusing to be purely animal,
would rouse yourself to say sardonic things.
We saw triumph in that, too, in your wit
and social graces, took comfort
in a weening pride and intellect
that lurked inside the face of a cadaver.

While you would be decorous to the end,
I cannot be—and though I mean no disrespect,
I dwell upon the vision that you made,
and feel that I became a student of your death,
learning a lesson I think you might approve:
to live in fear of Death, and live
extreme, unimpressed by his civilities.

Eros

Three days neglected
in the refrigerator
unopened in a brown paper bag.
Who would have thought
they could still be beautiful?
I must have done something right
by accident.

Raspberries in a white bowl:
red beehives with cream
beads on furry hills.
And those impossible yellow hairs
extending between the mounds!

I love using stuff up.
It always gives me the deepest pleasure.

Traveler's Notes

for Regina

When she heard I was going to France, my Aunt Regina said: "When you get there, take a lover." That's right, my uncle agreed. That's the way to learn a language. And, I think because she knew that she was dying, she said: "I have some more advice, my dear, though I don't mean to bore you. Two things I've always believed: Never postpone a pleasure, and never run to meet disaster." What if, I wondered, I couldn't tell the difference? "Well," she said smiling, "there's the difficulty."

I couldn't really say I knew her well. Maybe everyone's got a favorite aunt, one they don't often see, an exotic married into the family, and that family lucky for it. The day after Regina died I spent in bed—nothing I could recognize immediately as grief—I was just tired. I went out that night, a Saturday, to visit a friend, and on the way, in the supermarket, the *National Enquirer* announced this finding: "Human soul weighs 1/300,000th of an ounce! Scientists weigh bodies before and after death." I thought of Voltaire and his mistress in their bedchamber trying to weigh fire.

When I was in France—quite lonely, really, but determined to appear alone by choice—well-groomed, resilient, I went to Chantilly, and spent an afternoon on a guided tour of the château's interior, then took a walk into the grounds, among the flat pools and long lawns, gargantuan statuary that I tried to identify (the one I was sure of was Molière). And far away, carefully planted rows of dark trees that didn't limit the property, just emphasized its enormity. All around the château, reflected in a pool that circled it, a skirt of waters showed it like a mirror and reproduced the sky, which was, that day, all gray, the clouds white and gray, great puffs in constellations, flat upon the bottom, that seemed to be the border of another world—and that world, too, reflected in the pool undistortedly. I rested for a while, thought that if I lived there I would have stolen out at night to meet my lover, two floating shapes converging on some designated plot of grass and leaves somewhere beneath the trees. Then I got up—the guards were wanting to close the gates.

Beyond the gate there was a bridge lined with tourists who were straining from its reaches, throwing baguettes in chunks at fish. The fish were huge, their mouths and teeth distinct—their lips were fleshy and very pink. Hundreds of them, so fat, I didn't think their frenzy caused by hunger. Splashing and sliding the whole of their bodies against one another, over and then under, scales flashing iridescence, chasing any floating bit of bread, then fighting for it, breaking it up among them. Noisy in their greed, the way I've never known fish to be noisy, an odd grunt, astonished eyes protruding. Not greed, but beauty, and instinct. Regina, who was never insulted or surprised by her body's essay into frailty, would have liked it. We might have stood together among the tourists with our mouths gaping, eyes gaping at the fishes' gaping mouths, at the edge of the château where the force of world upon world narrowed the distinction between earth and sky.

Earthly Desires

Dream of a life of rustic gentility,
warm house, magnetic, not too big, but large enough
for French doors, sudden windows
at the turn of narrow stairs, view
of the thoughtful garden, just the glimpse
of dogwood as an understory, and so much light
and people come for the pleasure of it, to talk,
time to gather and cook together. Doors left
open, the climate mild enough, the hill terraced
and the neighbors' white garage at the top of the curve
almost visible. Modest, really, yet appearing larger—
not the only place, but the terra firma, the place one retired
after searching, or where one searched privately, between heroic forays.
Return in triumph. Astonishing facility. Hip hip.
Taking the moments of happiness to be just the beginning,
dream of the life that was always about to be like that
all of the time.

Home Range

Adjacent territories form
a patchwork (stippled and
hatched areas) that are often
three-dimensional,

1

so that
roofs, fences, or trees
may not necessarily
belong to the cat
whose territory is beneath.

Most home ranges
are limited
to the owner's garden or yard,
and may support
several cats
from the same household.

The territory of a female
or neuter

2

may be small
but is vigorously
defended,

3

particularly by a female
with kittens.
A tom

4

may command
an extensive area.

This may incorporate
part of the garden
of a no-cat household

5

that has been carved up
by neighboring cats.

A newcomer

6

confronts
these existing claimants
in trying to stake
its home range.

Cats sharing
territorial boundaries
or particular areas

7

within a multi-cat household
avoid conflict
by establishing
rights of way
at different times of day.

For the same reasons
communal highways

8

allow access
through closely juxtaposed
home ranges.

Areas not annexed
by any cat

may include
the territory
of a dog

9

and communal areas

10

sometimes only reached
by crossing the home range

11

of another cat.
Chance meetings
are often resolved

12

by a staring match.

Against the Old Government

Although you asked me to write a poem
about airports with a joke in it, and the word
t-e-a-r (you spelled it out)
in any of its forms, I would rather not.
You chose airports because I had talked
about them, about persuading my boyfriend
to take me to an airport
for my birthday. I was sixteen,
my boyfriend had taken me to dinner
somewhere in Chinatown, The Empress of China,
and a waiter had embarrassed me there:
he asked if I wanted a cocktail.
I wanted a cocktail, not to drink it,
just to see what it was like
to hold a cocktail in a public place
like an adult, when I was only sixteen.
Good, I thought, when the waiter asked,
You don't look sixteen.

I think now that it has always been this way:
the preoccupation with adulthood,
with doing the right thing; with
looking like you're doing the right thing.
Like going to the airport after dinner,
dressed in a subtly glamorous way,
glamour that made my age a mystery,
but an irrelevant mystery. I wished then
that I was wearing black sequins
and that I was running in long gorgeous strides
on my way to catch a plane,
my life so busy, my company so necessary
to this or that purpose — to important people.
But I was in the airport, pretending

to wait for a plane with my boyfriend,
wearing a necklace I didn't like much,
which was my birthday present.
I was sixteen. I wanted the world
to greet me. I wanted the world.

Letter to David

In the tinted photograph, the one I still keep,
You and I sit on the second of four steps,
Slightly away from one another, but touching
At the hip. That was a hot day.
We were dressed for church, I held an Indian doll,
And the concrete smelled stalely of the soles of shoes.
I had braids and you had a crew cut
We looked just like kids
And smiled into shapeless sunlight.

While you were away, I sent you poems
Not to create mystery, but to cheer you up.
I doubted they would reach you,
Not certain there was mail on sinking ships.
For weeks you believed they were sent by your wife.
Inspired by the faithfulness of poetic confession
You avoided the eyes of whores in Singapore and Saigon.
I was in college and you were at war
I thought that you would know me
By the Williams poem asking forgiveness
For eating the plums.

You buried yourself in the unfenced backyards of tract houses.
You began telling our father's stories with cloying aptitude.
I have been meaning to congratulate you:
On the phone, you two can't be told apart.
Master of the delayed reaction,
You drink the same beer in the same bars, mixing Budweiser
With Thorazine, Stelazine, Artane, Cogentin.
And once, when you were on the golf course,
The sloping mound of dichondra became

A pile of bloody bodies under your feet—
Human bodies tangled in unspeakable intimacies.

I have begun to suspect myself.
We have made careers of emotion.
Look, I mean to say
Insight is just fun for the moment.
It has no practical application.
You just need rules:
If your shooter is in the circle
Swap it with a cat's-eye or a three-toned molly;
Don't call this sickness;
Don't suffer: there is no virtue in it.

Focusing

Two wounds from cutting your hair: a blister
on the finger where the scissors worked,
and, on the other hand, a band-aid that conceals

a patch I snipped from another
finger's bending place. Small pains, to be sure,
not the stuff that operas are made of —

and I'm accustomed to this, too,
to the domestic smarts, the exposures
and reclosures of the homely arts.

These are minor trespasses, considering
the possibilities and my history of self-infliction.
Why, just weeks ago I fell down a flight of stairs,

launched like a toboggan from the top,
by the slippery sandals that I wore, exited the door,
and sailed toward eternity, saved by the intervention

of my rump. Off the crutches, finally,
when I was able to sit and drive again,
you asked after I had parked

if I could see in the dark,
and suggested that I wear my glasses.
"I'd have to look for them," I said. You held your tongue,

but the homily was clear; I heard as plain as day
what you refused to say: Women who wear glasses
don't get bumps on their asses.

Yesterday I remarked to a friend who noticed
that my finger did not bend, that I expected
every day I'd be wounded in some way — the effect

of an habitual circumscription. Years ago
I became resigned to see a hazy reverie,
years ago, in pain, stopped seeking out that clarity,

and gained and gained to blur the form
so that others might not see.
But now I confess there's a bone in my cheek,

and a waist begins to show
inside my dress—the body's visible.
I spent my mornings walking in the public passages

of private neighborhoods, talking to myself, disparaging
that happiness could last,
thinking about a fractious love

some distance in the past.
I envied everyone, and kept tabs on the neighborhood,
and saw myself gardening of a morning

in someone else's pasture, pruning neglected roses
in their yards, being better at their domestic chores,
quietly reproaching them

for a poorly chosen door, watching the progress
of someone's remodel, second-guessing and decrying
their lack of taste: "If it were my place . . ."

Under my nose there was someone
who kept his own counsel and thought himself
too far removed from my vision to appear.

One who had his loyalties all set but felt
himself divided—resignations of a kind
that only lucky blunders helped us find.

Ah Love, you're tired today, "really tired"
and I think of you to wish you stronger—
to ward off death or accident and keep you longer.

We wake in a garden, and though it's just a rental,
all that I hoped for crowds the lintel
and comes in. Yesterday,

on going to bed, I stepped in birdshit
in the dark, turned on the light,
and found a bird behind a pillow

on the floor, starkly out of place
and grabbed the cat and called to you to save it
if you could. It was a Stellar's jay,

the kind I once saw painted on a mural
near a park's concession stand,
and called "a thieving bandit." It's true,

they're social types, but this one
was alone, an accident in nature.
I couldn't tell which one he was,

or even if he was "he,"
(I hear that even experts disagree)
just one of many that we lure

to the peanut-cluttered windowsill
for early morning feedings.
We cultivate them shamelessly,

and like to think they like us, too;
There's wry and reckless theater
in the hollow thumping of their landings,

and the scratchy claws that click
as they hop sideways on the feeder,
then swoop and scrap and rush each other.

They seem to me the only birds with irony.
Alert and greedy,
with the reputation of a thief,

this might have been one of the larger jays
who likes to imitate the call of hawks,
then chokes a peanut down his throat

and takes another in his beak before diving off
to find some burying place.
Or he might have been the anxious one

who checks the heft and width of each peanut
with his beak, but cannot choose his meat.
He must have blundered in while dusk was falling,

and found himself entrapped in our domestic net
by accident. I felt sorry for him, too—
he was so out of place, without the cunning

I'd admired. He held his beak upright
in the posture of a newborn, as if waiting
for a feeding, or struggling to speak.

No sound came out. I worried
that his heart would burst—
I'd read once that the hearts of birds

beat perilously when trapped.
The cat suspected nothing,
and you took the bird

in two cupped hands (he offered no resistance)
and put him in the garden,
where alyssum and iris almost hid him. We don't know

if he lasted through the night,
you said he couldn't fly, wouldn't see in the dark —
but by the morning

he was gone. We watched him, though,
the two of us, until we slept.
We kept the window open.

Acknowledgments

Grateful acknowledgment is made to the editors of the following
publications in which the poems below first appeared.

Susan Aizenberg, *Peru*

AGNI, "Nights Mutable as Water Revise Themselves into the Shape of
  Our Extravagant Past"
The Connecticut Review, "Half-Light: No Feeling"
The Devil's Millhopper, "Grand Street"
Iowa Woman, "Cleaning the Bank"
The Journal, "The Life You Really Have"
Kalliope, "Winter Photograph of Brighton Beach, Brooklyn"
The Laurel Review, "Flying West"
Passages North, "Anniversary"
The Poetry Miscellany, "What It Is"
Prague Review, "Twenty-five Years from Anywhere Like That"
Prairie Schooner, "In the Frame," and "L'Heure Bleue"
Red Brick Review, "Paradise"
Spoon River Poetry Review, "Sometimes When You're Asleep"
Sun Dog: The Southeast Review, "Art"
Third Coast, "Luminous Child"

Heartfelt gratitude, for their invaluable help, to Michael David, Richard
Duggin, Art Homer, Richard Jackson, Roger Weingarten, and David
Wojahn; to Erin Belieu and Carol Lynn Marrazzo, *amigas de mi corazón*;
and to Lynda Hull, whose luminous spirit endures. Most special thanks
to Aaron, Christopher, and Jeffrey Aizenberg.

124

Mark Turpin, *Nailer*

AGNI, "Everything under the Sun," and "Downslope"
The Berkeley Poetry Review, "Nailer"
Boston Review, "The Box," "Pickwork," "Shithouse," "In Winter,"
    "Will Turpin b. 1987," and "Photograph from Antietam"
The Paris Review, "Pickwork," and "The Box"
Ploughshares, "Photograph from Antietam," and "Before Groundbreak"
The Threepenny Review, "Laborer's Code"

Suzanne Qualls, *Beauty, and Instinct*

AGNI, "Au Pair," "Encomium," and "The Wrong Son"
Boston Review, "Death of a Scholar," "Katie Can't Go Out Today," "Letter
    to David"
Occident, "Old Story" (under a different title), and "Home Range"
The Threepenny Review, "Early in a Rotten Summer"
Triquarterly, "Death of a Scholar"
Verse, "Laurie's Mother Back from the Dead"

This book was designed by Will Powers. It is set in Charlotte and Franklin Gothic type by Stanton Publication Services, Inc. and manufactured by BookCrafters on acid-free paper.

Cover design by Jeanne Lee.

.